STAY YOUNG

Reduce Your Rate of Aging

by
John Keith Beddow, Ph.D.

**A Book About Reducing
The Rate of Aging**

ISBN 0-9617531-0-2
Published by Shape Technology Limited
901 Park Place, Iowa City, Iowa 52240 U.S.A.
1986

DEDICATION

To my best friend, Joan.

CONTENTS

I. Aging Defined

So you are growing older? Well we are all growing older. After all it is a part of being alive. As every one of our days passes, we age by one day more. But do you *feel* that you are growing older? Think about it.

People usually reach a peak in their twenties, or so we are told. Thereafter it is all down hill. Do you feel that you are going down hill? Think about it.

Do you remember the day you were thirty-five? You looked at yourself in the bathroom mirror for signs of aging. There were no discernible gray hairs. True there was the odd "wrinkle" but it was due to a localized excess of fat rather than getting old, so it didn't count. No, at thirty-five there were no very obvious signs of aging. And you didn't feel older, either. So you concluded that although others may be aging, you were not (at least not very rapidly). But now that you are on the far side of thirty-five and you are experiencing aging you realize that your thoughts at thirty-five were erroneous. You were just plain wrong. But how so?

By now your hair is beginning to fall out — maybe you are balding. These are unmistakable signs of aging. "Hold on!" you say: "I know some guys who are bald before they are thirty-five, so baldness cannot be a sign of aging. Surely it is what the experts call "male pattern baldness." It is due to hormones, isn't it? Are you sure? Think about it.

Years ago you would accelerate when going up a short flight of three or four stairs. You would almost if not actually run up them. Now you walk sedately up stairs. Let the young bucks run up stairs — it's only a waste of energy anyhow. But don't you think that such thoughts are merely rationalizations? The fact is that whereas before you felt good and you wanted to run up those darn stairs, now at best, you just don't want to run up stairs. You just don't feel "peppy." Have you ever wondered why this is so? If this is aging, is it inevitable? Can you do anything about it?

Romance is in the air. Her skin glistens

in the candlelight. You are experiencing all sorts of risque thoughts. Can't wait to slurp that last tot of wine and haul this vision of voluptuousness off to bed. The problem nagging away at you is that once you get her there you can not *guarantee* an erection and a satisfying performance, at least on your part. Deary me, this is getting serious. If this is aging, it can undermine one's self confidence and self esteem. But more than that, if it messes up your love life, that's a disaster. So maybe you really will have to think about it. I know I did.

Just what is aging? Aging is very simply a process in which the rate of damage exceeds the rate of repair. By this definition, aging is a failure of the maintenance system of the body. If we think about aging in this way it offers the possibility of a methodology by which we can attempt to reduce the rate of aging. This is what this book is about: how you can go about the task of trying to reduce your rate of aging. In these pages I describe the information that I have come across and the thoughts that I have had about Aging Rate Reduction (ARR, for short). I will also describe some of the discipline I practice, some of the routines I follow. Read what follows as one man's attempt to slow down the inevitable. After all, all of us travel from birth to death. What one is trying to do is to make the journey as pleasant and non-terrifying as possible.

For quite some years now I have been carefully monitoring and controlling my habits in order to maintain a healthy physical and mental condition so that both family life and life in the workplace can be consistently rewarding. With the passage of time the focus of this interest has gradually shifted to an effort to reduce my rate of aging so that for the last five years I have been experimenting with various combinations of habits in order to develop a recognizable program of aging rate reduction — ARR for short.

The program itself consists essentially of a combination of fasting, diet control, exercise, vitamin and mineral intake, stress control and a good love life. The underlying principle of these efforts is to try to take better care of the warriors of my immunological system than before so that they can all the better defend me against those adversaries that would ravage me with age and disease.

Ravage? Is that not rather too strong a word? No, definitely no. Aging is truly an incurable disease that we all must go through. It ruins our physique, our minds, it forces us out of our life's work and ultimately out of our life. Each of us has heard of the idea about growing old gracefully. It is a beautiful thought. Unfortunately, it is not everybody's destiny as a visit to the county home, old folks hostel, the geriatric clinic or other appropriate location will show. As we all of us have to grow old, clearly we would prefer to do it gracefully. The purpose of the ARR program is to try to increase the probability that I will be able to do just that.

Being a person of modest talent, living a quiet life in a rather out of the way place, there would have been no attempt on my part to write a little book about my Aging Rate Reduction experiment except for something that occurred during a recent trip to Asia. On this trip I met four people in three different countries whom I know quite well but who had not seem me for approximately 12-18 months. In their various ways, all four quite independently and without prompting from me said that I looked younger. This was the first independent confirmation to me that my ARR program was working. I had already satisfied myself that it was working, but you can imagine how happy I was to receive the supportive opinions of others. In writing this little book, I am most conscious of a lack of knowledge of what I am about. But that is nothing new, that is what life is about — discovery and adventure; all the same I do feel constrained to point out that I am merely trying to tell my story. This book is not a claim to have discovered the fountain of youth. I believe that the ARR program outlined in this book is working for me. It, or a variant, might work for you. Then again, it might not. Don't try it if you think you'll get sick.

II. Aging Rate Reduction Program
Aging and Longevity

The really astute reader will have caught the implication that if one reduces the rate of aging, one should then be able to expect to live longer, barring accidents. True? Unfortunately, not necessarily so. This is because there are numerous schools of thought about the aging process. One view has it that we are programmed by a biological clock. According to this view, this clock just keeps on ticking away until a specific time has elapsed, at one point we reach puberty, at another our hair starts to fall out, etc., etc. . . . We can naturally expect to live until the Biblical three score and ten and the longevity of the populations of some of the more advanced countries is about equal to this seventy year mark. This tends to support the idea of the biological clock.

On the other hand when something unusual occurs in a population, such as the reduction of longevity in the male population of the Soviet Union, this tends to underscore the influence of environmental conditions upon the rate of aging. In the case of the Soviet Union the experts believe that heavy drinking and smoking by adult males is exacting a terrible toll on the nation's health. Although I accept that they all smoke and drink too much, it seems to me that blaming the decreased longevity on purely physical factors is rather simple-minded. The dominant influence in human evolution during the past two million years or so has been the influence of human society itself rather than the purely physical conditions of existence. This being so, I suspect that the dominant factor in determining longevity is the societal factor. In short, we have to learn when to die. *Longevity is a learned behavior.* This viewpoint helps explain why the reduction in Russian longevity is so sudden. My paternal grandfather died two days after my grandmother. You can say that he died of a broken heart. It is said that the aborigines of Australia look o.k. and feel fine right up until the day they go. They pop off more or less when they are expected to.

No one can deny that there are extremely heavy pressures upon people to "step aside." In the United States there are many retirement programs plus the whole social security apparatus. All of these are geared to moving people out of the work force and out of the real world. In fact, the longer we live the more of an expense to society we become. Witness the clamor about the cost of health care for the aged. Some years ago in a fit of paternalistic fever, the U.S. Congress enacted a compulsory retirement age for all of the working U.S. population. This evoked a huge outcry. The Americans were saying that they were changing their minds about when to die. As they evidently intended to live longer than before, being forced to retire at a specific age (and too young) would hinder the aspirations of the population. The one exception in the whole land to this is the stricture that University Professors shall retire at 70. It appears that one can carry out brain surgery until one is 90 but one is not permitted to teach it after one attains 70 years of age!

The bottom line in the above discussion is that if you want to live longer then you are on your own. Nature wants you to live just

long enough to raise your family. Society
wants you to live a little bit longer than that
so you can certainly occupy living space and
consume until around about 70. Then you
must go! I know what you are thinking —
women live longer than men. Yes, they do indeed. But they are more discreet and tolerant.
They hide their needs and thoughts from the
bulk of society and work through members of
their family — or they did until a short while
ago! Since the women's lib thing, women are
imposing themselves on society more than
they did. If my idea is right, there will be increasing pressure on women to "step aside."
Before going on, let's just collect our ideas
together:

• The rate of aging and the age at death are
  most likely linked, but the strength of the
  linkage depends upon the individual and his
  circumstances. For example, if you could
  (hypothetically) reduce your rate of aging by
  50%, would you expect to live twice as long?
  I think not. And therefore though you
  hopefully expect to live longer if you reduce
  your rate of aging — there is no guarantee.
  ARR is something of a personal experiment.
  In short, you are doing research on yourself.

Isn't that nice!

- Longevity is socially controlled to an important extent that varies with the type of society.
- The rate of aging and also the age at death can be influenced by the degree of prudence that a man exerts. For example, if you like to drive racing cars at 200 miles per hour, then you are not being very prudent and don't expect to live too long. The same goes for the chain smoker and the habitual drunk. It is reasonable to believe that if our anticipated age at death is say 70 years, then we can influence the variance on this by the way in which we live. In other words: expect to live to 70 years + 15 years. What this means is that if you are prudent, you may live as long as 70 + 15 = 85 years old. On the other hand, if you live your life like a big slobbering toad, maybe you will depart as young as 70 - 15 = 55 years of age. Then again, how old one dies at may be just the luck of the draw. Who knows? However, this approach to the problem does give us a target to aim for: to reduce our rate of aging such that we extend our life span from say 70 to 85 years of age.

The target seems to be a modest one. We are not seeking to live until the 125 year age mark. That would necessitate overcoming the societal pressure mentioned earlier. Clearly the 85 year target is attainable (if at all) mostly by more prudent living. The more wily among you will already have caught the nasty drift which is: more prudent living is going to require some discipline. In my own case, my maternal and paternal grandfathers and also my father all died in their early 70's. Clearly, if I am going to reduce my rate of aging and correspondingly lengthen my life to 85 years or so, I am going to have to pull something big out of the bag. (Maybe the third time will be lucky!) "Yes," I can hear you say, "but what?"

Aging Rate Reduction

Aging Rate Reduction is achieved by an individual man when he practices a focused and regularly disciplined way of life. This discipline has six essential components to it. These are:
• Fasting
• Diet

- Exercise
- Vitamins and Minerals
- Stress Control
- No Funny Habits

No! No! It is not a formula for a miserable life! Nor does being prudent have anything to do with being a prude! I practice the ARR discipline. I am 54 years of age. I lead a very happy and joyful, productive life. I'm happily married to the same woman for 30 years and we have four children. I have been blessed with good health in my adult years except for odd bouts of Asian Flu, Hong Kong Flu, and the occasional accident (once I actually ran into a tree).

If you have never really bothered very much with any components of the ARR Discipline, then I suggest that starting off on all six of them simultaneously will probably kill you off, and quickly. Better to take it ever so gradually. Learn to "listen" to your body. If you feel tired, go to sleep. A twenty minute snooze at the right time is the equivalent of a tax-free, no-risk, capital gain. It is pure and instantaneous profit.

In the pages that follow you will read of what I practice. You will learn why I do what

I do and what the consequences seem to be that I detect in my own person. Also, how this affects others in my family and friends and colleagues. If you want to adopt or adapt any part of this program of ARR Discipline, then good luck to you, sincerely. But keep in mind that you do so at your own risk. It is yourself that you are experimenting with.

III. A Reassurance

Ah! The suspicious mind! "Does this guy practice what he preaches?" Well I am certainly trying to preach what I practice. Just to set your mind at rest: I have been fasting for just over five years. Experiments with food intake have been going on for about 14 years. I have been exercising on a more or less regular basis since 1942 by dint of running approximately 2½ - 3 miles per day. I laid off for four or five years at one point. My mother used to make me take a cod liver oil capsule when I was a child, so I suppose that taking vitamins has been a regular part of my life. All the same, I have focused more carefully on this component during the last 20 years. The development of a methodology to control stress has been something that I have worked at for many years now. Let's estimate that 25 years on an on-again-off-again basis with some success after the forties began. Fun habits? JKB has been known to smoke, to take a drink and to overeat (I love eating). But once I commenced the ARR these practices have been closely controlled or completely cut out. By the way — absolutely no drugs. Life is complicated and hard enough without one having to drag around a big, heavy chain with one. Incidentally, my blood pressure is nicely below average and my pulse rate is also low.

IV. Fasting
Aging

Fasting means going without food for a specified period of time. It has been practiced since early times. It has been used for religious purposes in connection with death rites including mourning and it has also been used in fertility rites. Formal religions practice fasting in some form or another and indeed the early Christian Saints were well known for their fasting practices. These were often associated with penance.

So! Why should we be interested in fasting? Certainly not for the purpose of becoming a saint. Saints are overly preoccupied with the next world and I am rather more interested in this one. Why, then, bring the matter up? Because it is, I believe, a necessary prerequisite and concommitant of the ARR strategy. Without fasting, I doubt that aging rate reduction can be optimally achieved or perhaps even achieved at all.

The idea of using the technique of fasting to achieve a reduction in one's rate of aging might seem a little outlandish and maybe even bizarre at first glance, so the following is an account of how I figured it out. Laboratory rodents, rats and mice, are traditionally used in life science experiments to avoid the necessity of putting humans through the pain and discomfort of the experiment and also because of genetic advantages gained from using the rodents. In addition, the investigator can conduct an autopsy on the rodent to find out what happened. Clearly one cannot do this with people (shades of Dr. Moreau). Because of the obvious differences between rodents and people it is often something of a conjecture as to what rodent experiments might mean for us. All the same there is one fasting experiment on laboratory animals that when coupled with some elementary knowledge of the latest scoop on the theories of aging is one of the greatest significance for ARR. When I first heard of the fasting experiment and thought about it for a day or two, its importance hit me like a ton of bricks. In the experiment reported on PBS in a documentary, the rodents were divided up into three groups. Members of one group were allowed to eat whatever was available whenever they felt like eating. Members of this group aged rapidly and died off way ahead of the other two groups. The second group was put on a strict regime diet so that each and every day members of this group got sufficient food and no more. This group lived a lot longer than the first group but the members of this group aged more rapidly than those in the third group. This third group was fed a strict regime diet every odd day and was starved every even day. That is to say members of the third group of animals were forced to fast every other day and when they did eat, they ate a strict regime diet. Needless to say this third group lived much longer than the second group. And of course, they lived much, much longer than the first group that more or less ate itself into an early grave. This is very significant as it indicates that fasting can promote a reduced rate of aging and prolong life. What is also very interesting is that members of this third group were jumping around "like two-year-olds" when members of the second group were loafing around all humped up with age.

There we have it! Fasting in rats can extend life and reduce the rate of aging! The big question is why? The really BIG question is (even if we cannot explain it): is the result transferable or applicable to humans? In short, can I do it for (or is it to?) myself? The answer is yes. I am fasting and I believe that it is working for me. Incidentally, the rodent fasting experiment was first conducted more than a quarter of a century ago. It was more recently repeated with the same result. But hold it! Just because some mad scientist has starved a bunch of rats into submission, let's not go off the deep end. The real clincher comes when you consider the rat fasting in conjunction with the free radical theory of aging.

When we undergo aging, it means that the individual cells of our body are each in their own ways undergoing aging. I am the sum total of all my cells. As they get older and age, then so do I. Earlier we mentioned the biological clock aspect of aging. There is another, perhaps more important, idea about aging called the *free radical theory of aging*. Free radicals are chemically active units which roam freely around the body. They become attached to parts of our cells, either inside or on the surface. In these locations, the attached free radicals can hinder the effective cell functioning. Eventually if the free radicals were not removed, the cells would choke up and cease to operate. The process of getting choked up is what we call aging. Fortunately our body has the means to fight off and remove these freebooters. This cleansing is carried out by our immunological system.

Immunological System

Our immunological system defends our body from outside attack and it also cleans it up. The agents in all of this are the white blood cells. The system is so fantastic! Its story is one of the most incredible and at the same time one of the more exciting ones that one can possibly read. A brief outline is as follows: there are two main classes of cells — phagocytes and lymphocytes. The phagocytes are the general infantry of the immune system. If a phagocyte finds some alien bozo in its vicinity, there's a fight to the death. Either the phagocyte wins and the alien in-

vader is destroyed or the phagocyte is killed
off. But what is one phagocyte among so
many? There are literally billions of them. The
body produces them in the marrow and stores
them in local sinuses. When our body is in-
vaded a chemical trumpet sounds and a truly bloody war of extermination ensues. One
common phagocyte is called a neutrophil. This
is a small but valiant defender. They also clean
up debris and so though valiant, they are not
too proud (unlike the knights of old). A much
more formidable phagocyte is the
macrophage. This starts out life as a smaller
monocyte, but transforms to the larger and
fiercer macrophage when it senses a battle in
the offing. The word "macrophage" means
"big eater." These cells are not the sort of
thing you would want to meet if you didn't
belong. Macrophages also clean up the
system. They are capable of reproduction and
they can live for a period of years. Think about
it, instead of buying a dog or a cat, adopt instead one of your own (your very own)
macrophages. Give it a pet name — how about
"Big John"?

The other cells, the lymphocytes, are more
specialized. They are akin to special forces in-

sofar as they go after specific invaders once they are triggered off. The lymphocytes constitute about one quarter of all the white blood cells. There are two main types of lymphocytes — B-cells and T-cells. The B-cells make antibodies to fight specific invading disease organisms. The T-cells are happiest when they are out and about killing off tumor cells. The lymphocyte story is a very complicated one. The name for the invader is an antigen. The appearance of an antigen spurs a hostile response from the appropriate B-cell or T-cell. The gland called the thymus, which is located behind the breast bone, is partially responsible for T-cell behavior. The thymus appears to influence the development of T-cells. As someone put it, "the T-cells get their marching orders from the thymus." If you have always thought that the defenders die young, then think again. The average life of a T-cell is 4½ years, which is not bad for an individual on call 24 hours a day and fighting permanently in the trenches. I remember a veteran of the First World War telling me that he had gone "over the top" (that is out of the trench into no-man's land to fight the enemy) four times. He told me there were very few men who ever survived four times. Consequently he was joyful and content with his life even though he had breathing difficulty due to having been gassed with mustard gas. It is surprising to learn that some of the T-cells of our body live for up to twenty years. So rather than adopt them as pets, why not as a relative?

To summarize: our body possesses an immunological system that defends us from alien attack and also keeps our cells and body clean. These warriors protect us from invading bacteria and viruses. They attack and destroy cancer cells and they remove and clean out anything that does not belong — for example, a well-entrenched former free radical.

Hypotheses of Aging

So, the working hypothesis of aging that I have adopted is that the major milestones are probably determined by the society in which we find ourselves living. The smaller variation is influenced by how prudently we live. The big question is how does this all fit in with the fasting routine? It appears to me to be rather simple. The rodents that were starved every other day did not take in anything during their off days other than air and water. Therefore, the lowered load on the immunological system allowed a mopping-up operation to take place. One would expect that in normal circumstances (eating every day) that the immunological warriors would defend and clean up with customary gusto. However, there is always the chance that *not quite all* of the odd bits and pieces would be eradicated from the cells of the body. This remnant would, over the course of the years, build up and impair the normal functions. This is the process of aging. Note also that the impaired cells would pass on their impairment when reproducing, so that once started the process is difficult to stop. Moreover, it has the mathematics of a catastrophe which is after all what aging is. Quite naturally, if people overindulge with eating, drinking or whatever, then they overtax the immunological system and the remnant is bigger in proportion to what it would have been if these same people had been more temperate in their habits. Now consider the effect of fasting: in this case when the body is being fed, all operates as usual. When the individual is fasting, the immunological system can really clean house. Consequently the remnant is smaller than is the case without fasting. To my way of thinking, this is plain common sense.

My Fasting Experiments

An important question is: exactly how much fasting is enough? The true answer to this question is that nobody knows. I will recount my own experience so that the reader can judge for himself. Originally, I started trying to fast three days per week. I would cease eating at about 8 pm Sunday night and refrain from eating for all of the following day, Monday. Breakfast at 8 am on Tuesday morning was something of an event the first week I started the fasting experiment. In truth, I was not overly civilized when someone got in my way in the kitchen. A day of starvation concentrates the mental energies on food quite wonderfully. I was ravenous and probably subliminally growling. Based on this experience, my advice to any man that fasts is to have your breakfast on your own for the first few mornings. This will certainly help you keep peace in the home. It may also help to keep you on an unswerving fasting track too.

On this first routine, I fasted on Monday, Wednesday, and Friday. All went well for a while. This period went on for a few months, probably four or five months. In the end it did not suit me. Perhaps it was a combination of factors that put me off. In the first place, it meant that every Monday was the same food-wise as every other Monday. This in itself was a little bit boring. In addition, it is nice every now and again to eat one's fill on Friday, the last working day of the week. It finishes the work week off; it's a sort of reward to have dinner on Friday evening. The next step was to reduce the fasting to two days per week. In this case Monday and Thursday. The advantage of this new method was that it kept Friday as an eating day. The disadvantage was that it was monotonous plus it did not really seem to be working. I did not actually feel any different. I was just missing two dinners per week and getting pretty mad about it too.

After about 18 months of experimenting with different variations of the fasting routine

I decided that more or less drastic action was required to get the result that I was looking for. What was I looking for? I wanted to end, and if possible, reverse a trend that had been disturbing me. For a while I had been acquiring a feeling of being satisfied with things. It might be best called a feeling of complacency. It is a very dangerous feeling for a man to have at any age but it is especially dangerous at 50. To be honest I was very frightened by this feeling of complacency and especially scared of its potential and very likely consequences.

The Fasting Routine I Use

I wanted to re-establish a mental attitude and a physical capability to back it up such that having made a decision to do something I could then go and do it and *would actually do so.* For some time previously I had noticed a reluctance to do things creeping up on me; an unwillingness to "make the effort"; a lack of commitment to the task of living my life as I had previously done. In short I was being overtaken and undermined by a creeping, enervating complacency. It occurred to me that this had something to do with aging and it was this feeling more than anything else that prompted my interest in ARR.

It was June of 1982 (I think!) that the decision was made to change the fasting routine to match that of the rodent fasting experiment. After all, I thought to myself, humans are a lot like rats. And in any case I knew it wouldn't kill me. Not right away, that is. The fasting routine was switched to every other day and it has proved most satisfactory and successful.

The Results

After three and one-half years of practice it can now be revealed that I have forsaken more than 600 dinners and breakfasts! But that is just about the only negative aspect of the whole experiment. Some of the benefits include:
- the feeling of creeping complacency has entirely departed.
- my general energy level is higher and consistently so.
- my interest and capability for starting new projects is much increased.

- productivity is high.
- my ability to engage in battle with folks farther up the line has recovered.
- there is no problem sleeping and taking a nap is much easier.
- on the days when I fast my feeling is one of taking a rest.
- my love life is much improved and consistent.

But nothing is gained at zero costs. There are some debits, some disadvantages. One of the more noticeable drawbacks occurs when one is out at dinner with friends on a fast day. Frankly, I feel like a chump. On the other hand in the privacy of one's own home, it is very easy to sit at the dining table and extol the virtues of abstinence while everyone else is stuffing his or her face. Life is full of little pleasures. On a more serious note, it was very early on noticed by my wife that there had occurred a partial reversion of personality to what I had been like in my 30's and 40's. What this means is that I became "quicker on the draw" and not willing to suffer fools as gladly as before. It was necessary to learn how to trim these sails of mine and things have more or less settled down at home. All the same, it does not do to make a strong challenge when I'm on my own turf.

Yet another potentially serious problem seems to have something to do with blood sugar level. Approximately two years ago I had come into the house from my work on a fast day. I decided to make myself a drink of hot chocolate and sweetened it with sugar. Soon after starting to sip the drink a feeling of nausea welled up within me. My ears began to feel as though they were filling with water and I started to sweat profusely. All of this occurred whilst I was sitting quietly in an easy chair. The beads of sweat rolled down my face and grew into rivulets which dripped and ran off my nose and chin onto the carpet. I could not get up and walk to the bathroom because of feeling too weak to do so. In any case it seemed best to just continue to sit there quietly and wait for the situation to right itself. Eventually the sweating stopped and all other adverse reactions faded away. During conversations with various people some hinted darkly at diabetes, others muttered about hypoglycemic shock. Whatever the problem, it has since been avoided by the rather simple expedient of sucking a hard-boiled sweet (containing sugar) every now and then during the course of a fast day. I reckon that the day of the fainting attack, my blood sugar was extremely low, so that the intake of heavily sugared hot chocolate (plus, perhaps the caffeine booster in the chocolate) was a bit of a shock for my system. Anyway, it has not happened again. One question that must have occurred to you is how it feels when one fasts. The answer to that is simply why not try it and find out for yourself? This is not a flippant answer. Each and every one of us differs. In the experience just related, I explained how neither a three day per week, nor a two day per week routine worked for me. It has been necessary for me to go the "whole hog" and fast every alternate day. However, please be warned because fasting for only a day is sometimes more than a person can stand. For example a friend and colleague of mine experiences some dizziness when he fasts for a day. Also he says that it affects his ability to work creatively and at high pressure. The answer to that one is to fast at the weekend. And in any case, one does not work creatively all of the time, let's face it.

And So

There is certainly a feeling of inner peace and rest when fasting and if one can survive quite comfortably eating on every other day, why do people persist in eating on each and every day of their lives? I think the answer to that is for human beings eating has something of a sacramental quality to it. For us, eating meals together is one of the most important social activities of our lives. It is not every day that we engage in deep and philosophical conversation, but most of us do sit down for meals together and daily. I have noticed that even on the days when fasting, I will sit at the family meal table and interact. The other main reason for eating every day of our lives is to please the farmer. When all is said and done, we are literally processing his produce. Also for most of us eating is a great physical pleasure. Fasting is therefore a process in which one gives up the pleasure of the moment for a tangible but perhaps elusive goal. The bottom line is this: I have been following an every other day fasting routine for three and one half years now. I am very, very much satisfied with the results and barring unforeseen circumstances I do not believe that I shall return to a daily eating routine in the future. By the way, apart from an initial weight loss, the body adjusts soon enough so fasting is not a good way to control one's weight.

V. Eating
Fussy Eaters

The structure of a human being is very interesting. A great deal of our energy goes to fuel the activity of our brain. The importance of our brain is further indicated by the fact that we carry it just as far away from the ground as we possibly can. After all, the ground is rather dirty and it can be dangerous. So there we are with our brain encased in its bony box on the top of our torso. When the brain wants to go somewhere, the orders go out and lo! the legs stretch forth, our hips wiggle a bit and we have moved! But it is even more interesting than that. One of the major preoccupations is eating, but the brain is in no way going to permit the body to gobble just any old bit of food it happens to find. In order to make doubly sure, the sense organs are tightly packed around the brain. Just think, if you want to consume food, it has to be brought toward the mouth by sensitive nerve-laden hands. Near the mouth the eyes, nose and finally the tongue carefully examine the food.

These organs are directly connected to the brain. If a signal is received that indicates something is wrong, the food can be rejected. In other words, the food must pass a sight test, a smell test, and a taste test before it is consumed. This is surely a fine example of quality control. It is both elementary and crucial to our good health and it has played no small part in our evolutionary success.

There is one aspect of human behavior that always puzzled me for many years until I made the connection with food selection/rejection outlined above. Consider for a moment the interesting scenario in which you have supervised the manufacture of a particular product. You have all of the test data that has been generated by the many sophisticated tests that the product has just been run through. There is no doubt that the product is up to scratch. It is well within specification. There is one small flaw — it looks just a little bit off. There are a couple of scratches and scuff marks on the top surface. I can guarantee that no matter what you say, no matter how hard you protest, it will be almost impossible to sell the product. You may be able to get rid of it by drastically cutting the price. But the fact remains that almost every potential purchaser will reject your product, *even though they know full well that it is perfectly o.k.* except for the scuff marks. This is quite remarkable behavior and I believe that it is a direct result of the strong, built-in instinct for survival that we have evolved with. Because our senses locate the flaw in a product that is new it matters little what the test data and salesman's assurances are, we instinctively and strongly reject. Why is this important and what has it got to do with eating and diet? A moment's thought will make one realize that we are descended from a long line of fussy eaters. Otherwise we would not have survived at all. And we continue to be fussy eaters as witnessed by the pervasive interest in food, food hygiene, cooking, gourmet eating and all the rest of the paraphernalia associated with our appetite. What are the survival benefits of being a fussy eater? Indeed are there any such benefits or is a fussy eater merely a pansy?

I do not like burnt toast. It is true that a great deal of toast burning goes on when I'm in the kitchen doing my thing. However, I just don't like it and scrape it off with monotonous regularity. Apart from avoiding the funny taste, what could possibly be the survival value in scraping the toast? Just this: the burnt materials contain a large variety of DNA damaging chemicals and other chemicals that most probably have carcinogenic properties. That is to say, the burnt offering on your toast contains both mutagenic and carcinogenic materials. You most certainly do *not* want to have such materials in your diet if you can possibly avoid them. During the past 60 years or so there has occurred a steady reduction in the incidence of stomach cancer in the United States. The main reason for this steady and sizeable decline is believed to be due to the improvement in the treatment of meat. Animals are processed in relatively hygienic conditions and most importantly, the meat is frozen and refrigerated all along the remainder of the food distribution chain. There has been a decline in the incidence of blue mold on meat and as the mold is carcinogenic, its decline has been accompanied by a parallel reduction in the incidence of stomach cancer. So it really does pay to be rather careful what you eat.

A Balanced Diet

It is true to say that we are what we eat. It may be more accurate to say that we are made out of what we eat. Experts harangue us to eat "a balanced diet." The idea behind this stricture is that if we eat a little bit of this and a little bit of that, sooner or later we get all of the things that we need. Strong upholders of this approach would maintain that we do not need any supplementary vitamins or minerals, just a healthy well-balanced diet. They may well be right. I like to think that some time, long, long ago when the world was a simpler and more charming place, it was possible to eat a balanced diet. Now I'm not so sure. But there is a much, much deeper and indeed more sinister meaning to the idea of a balanced diet. Your diet — all of that nice food that you eat is stuffed full of goodies but it is also replete with carcinogens, mutagens and teratogens. On the bright side there are many natural antimutagens and anticarcinogens in our diet. Consequently, *the fundamental meaning of a balanced diet is to ensure that there are enough protective substances in the food to balance against those that might harm us.* The more obvious meaning is one that has been known for some time — to obtain all of the necessary vitamins and minerals along with calories sufficient for the day. One immediate consequence of this is that it might be considered unwise to eat all of one type of food at one period of the day and all of another type at another period. Such imbalances mitigate against both the superficial and deeper meaning of the need for a balanced diet.

What are the sources of these harmful substances? What are they? How do they act? Are there any antidotes? Are the antidotes in the same food as the harmful substances? If not, can one obtain supplemental supplies of antidotes? We cannot possibly answer all of these questions here, but we will learn enough to forage carefully and safely for ourselves.

Disease

It is our objective to reduce our rate of aging and this probably means that we will live longer and die later than we might otherwise have done. One of the major problems of growing older is the increased risk of getting cancer of some form or another. About 30% of people have cancer by the time they reach 85 years of age. Whereas in the past our forebears were carried off by disease at a more tender age, the longer we live the more likely it is that something will go wrong inside our own system. In fact cancer increases with the fourth power of age. In the case of mice, they attain the magic 30% cancer rate by the end of their short 2-3 year life span. This fact coupled with their genetic similarity to man makes mice particularly attractive for research subjects.

Toxins

Many of the mechanisms of aging, cancer, heart disease, and other diseases are related to the action of oxygen radicals which are generated as a result of the consumption of certain foods. Plants do not have hands and feet to defend themselves against predators; instead they conduct a complex and sophisticated chemical warfare using all manner of toxins that they generate specifically for defensive purposes. We eat a lot of plant materials — fruit and vegetables — in our normal diet. These various toxins are the subject of much study and debate. Their actions are complex but they all work on essentially the same basis. We are made up more or less of carbon-based molecules' with some hydrogen, oxygen and a few other bits and pieces tacked on. Such organic molecules are very prone to oxidation, a process which breaks up or otherwise disables the molecules functionality. This process eventually impairs the structure and behavior of affected cells. The toxins in our food tend to act through the generation of oxygen radicals which move into the cells of the body and do their damage. It is believed that this damage results in killer diseases that we tend to associate with people as they get older, such as cancer and heart disease.

Fat

We eat a great deal more than greens and fruit. One of the major suspects in the diet of western people is fat, especially rancid fat and fatty acids oxidized in other ways. It is estimated that more than 40% of the calories of the average western diet is made up of fat. The almost certain way of ensuring that this fat is oxidized to rather harmful products is to cook it. The nasty results include DNA damaging materials and mutagens and carcinogens produced in relatively substantial quantities. Two items are worthy of special notice: a sure sign of fat oxidation is the accumulation of lipofuscin in the tissue. Lipofuscin is associated with aging; it is the cause of the liver spots or aging spots that appear on the skin of elderly persons in areas exposed to the sun. The lipofuscin is a yellow pigment which not only occurs in the skin due to aging but also forms in the brain as a result of lipid peroxidation of the freely available unsaturated fat found therein (the proverbial fathead is not so rare!).

Yet another source of unpleasantness is the burnt and browned material produced by our so-called cooking. In fact the burnt and brown material on cooked protein is much more than unpleasant, it is highly mutagenic. Burnt toast, caramelized sugars, fried pork or bacon all introduce numerous DNA damaging substances and mutagenic materials into the diet. On this score, coffee beans are roasted and in consequence, a drink of coffee is a more or less sure way of ingesting a goodly dose of mutagenic materials.

Fat is a major risk factor in heart disease, colon cancer, breast cancer and various other health-related problems as outlined above. This, coupled with the greens and fruits toxins discussed earlier ought to make one very conscious of the fact that we are essentially a small, mobile chemical processing plant. Because we are biological we are capable of self-repair, assuming we look after ourselves. Also, because we are biological, we are vulnerable to insidious sorts of damage that gradually accumulate and interact with each other as we grow older. These effects are naturally gradual and are often either unnoticed by us or we grow accustomed to them and then do not notice until it is too late. Each of us therefore has a clear choice: one can live a lifestyle that lets tomorrow take care of itself and eat, drink and be merry. Alternatively, one can take reasonable precautions and make a serious effort to eat a healthy and well balanced diet. What constitutes a healthy and well balanced diet? I believe that the best way to answer this question is to take careful note of the food items that are somewhat unsafe for reasons already explained. Then we will review the agents that can help defend us against the harmful substances. The rest is up to you.

It's Us

We are so accustomed to blaming "them" for almost everything that it has become extremely popular to see environmental pollution as being almost entirely responsible for all our ills. To this frame of mind it must come as something of a shock to learn that the normal healthy food that we eat contains substances that literally do us in. Indeed, the toxins listed in Table 1 (page 46), indicate that the daily intake of "nature's pesticides" may amount to several grams each and every day that we eat. This should be compared and contrasted with the dietary intake of man-made pesticides amounting to one ten-thousandth of this. The man-made pesticide is relatively under control. Unless we observe a prudent dietary posture, our intake of natural

John Keith Beddow, Ph.D.

Table 1
HARMFUL SUBSTANCES IN THE DIET

Harmful Substances

Substances	Effect	Food Source
Safrole	Carcinogens in rodents. Metabolites are mutagens	Oil of sassafras used in sarsparella, rootbeer
Safrole and Piperine	Piperine causes tumors in mice	Black pepper. Estimated consumption is 140 mg/day.
Hydrazines	Lung tumors in mice, also stomach tumors	Edible mushrooms.
Glycoalkaloids	Can cause death, also teratogens.	When potatoes are diseased, bruised or exposed to light they turn brown and should not be eaten.
Quinones and phenol precursors, catechol	Make carcinogens, mutagens by oxidation	Rhubarb and mold toxins. Catechol derived from metabolism of plants. Derivatives occur in coffee.
Theobromine	DNA damage, testicular atrophy, sperm abnormalities in rats.	Cocoa powder.
Pyrrolizidine	Carcinogenic, mutagenic and teratogenic. Can cause lung and liver lesions.	Herbs and herbal teas.
Vicine, convicine	Sensitive people get severe hemolytic anemia.	Broad beans.

46

Table 1 (continued)

Substances	Effect	Food Source
Allyl isothiocyanate	Chromosome aberrations in hamster cells, cancers in rats.	Major flavor ingredient in oil of mustard and horseradish.
Gossypol	Damages human testes. Produces abnormal sperm and male sterility. Also causes skin cancer in mice.	Cottonseed oil. Toxin level depends on degree of refinement of oil.
Sterculic and Malavalic acids.	Various toxic effects in farm animals; carcinogens in trout; atherosclerosis in rabbits.	Found in cottonseed oil. Also in kapok, okra, durian. May also be found in fish, eggs, poultry and milk from animals fed on cottonseed oil.
Anagyrine	Teratogens causing birth defects in animals foraging on lupine. Can affect others in the same food chain — e.g., goat's milk.	Legumious plants such as lupine upon which grazing animals forage.
Phorbal Esters	Potent Carcinogens	Folk remedies and herbal teas.
Canavaniene	Causes a severe lupus erythematosus-like syndrome in monkeys fed on alfalfa sprouts.	Alfalfa sprouts are a significant source of this toxin. Lupus in humans is a serious immune system defect.
Aflatoxin and Sterigmatocystin	Mold carcinogens. They are among the most potent and deadly known.	Mold contaminated food such as corn, grain, nuts, peanut butter, bread, cheese, fruit, apple juice.

47

Table 1 (continued)

Substances	Effect	Food Source
Nitrosamines, nitrate, nitrate	Perhaps related to stomach and esophageal cancer.	Beets, celery, lettuce, spinach, radishes, and rhubarb.
Alcohol	Associated with cancer of mouth, esophagus, pharynx, larynx, and liver. Potent teratogen, leads to mental disorders of babies of mothers who drink.	Metabolized alcohol makes acetaldehyde — a mutagenic and teratogenic toxin.
Fat	High fat content in diet related to cancer and heart disease.	Rancid fat, or lipid peroxidation exposes the colon and digestive tract to many fat-derived carcinogens. Perioxisomes oxidize ingested fatty acids. This leads to the production of a host of DNA damaging compounds plus carcinogens and teratogens.
Burnt and browned materials	DNA damage, carcinogens, mutagens produced.	Cooked food including protein, sugars, bread, etc.
Methylglycoxal, chlorogenic acid.	Mutagenic effects, the acid has an anti-nitrosating effect.	Coffee
Cooked fats	See fat above	Cooking accelerates the rancidity reaction.

---

pesticides is way out of control. One can rightly ask if this is so serious. Or is it after all merely another faddish example of scaremongering? The answer to this is that the toxins listed in Table 1 do exist, we do eat them and they may very likely be associated with the effects described. Furthermore, a major cause of death in Japan is stomach cancer. This is not the case in the west and one would be hard put to ascribe the numerous cases of stomach cancer to anything other than dietary habit. In the west we die with heart attacks and other forms of cancer. But these health problems are also related to the same type of causes as are the stomach cancers of Japan.

The U.S. National Academy of Sciences has suggested that we reduce the fat content of our diet. Others suggest increasing the fibrous, fruit and vegetable content of our diet and reducing alcohol intake. Doubting Thomases will say that the definitive scientific proof is not yet in. My answer to that is that a similar type of person has been saying the very same thing about cigarette smoking and all the while smokers have been dying off with lung cancer and bad hearts.

I believe that where your health and safety are concerned, a nod's as good as a wink. Better to run scared than not to run at all.

Anticarcinogens

One of the most obvious methods of self-protection is to get rid of the damaged or affected tissue. This the body does in a more or less regular way by the shedding of the surface layer of our skin, stomach, intestines, colon and cornea.

We learned in the discussion above that oxygen radicals and lipid peroxidation are major factors in DNA damage. Protection against these and other oxidative processes can offset the unwelcome results to an extent that depends on many variables of diet and metabolism specific to each individual. But all is not despair because the same food that contains the substances that can harm us also contains other substances that offset the harm the others do and so offer some level of protection. These protective substances include Vitamin E, beta-Carotene, selenium, glutathione, ascorbic acid, uric acid and some edible plants.

Vitamin E (or tocopherol) acts as the major radical trap in lipid membranes. It also protects the body against carcinogens, mutagens and cardiac damage. Some protection against radiation induced DNA damage has been observed. Very heavy exercise can cause extensive oxygen radical damage to tissues in rats. It has been found that Vitamin E markedly increases the endurance of rats taking very heavy exercise.

Beta-Carotene is another extremely important antioxidant in the diet. It too acts as a free radical trap. It is especially efficient in trapping singlet oxygens which are particularly active in lipid peroxidation and are in themselves mutagenic. Carrots and all food containing chlorophyl contain beta-carotene.

Selenium is a very important element that significantly inhibits the start of skin, liver, colon, and mammary tumors in laboratory animals. There is evidence that selenium may contribute to heart problems.

Dietary glutathione is one of the more important antioxidants and antimutagens that occurs in the soluble fraction of cells.

Ascorbic acid is another major antioxidant that has been demonstrated to have important anticarcinogenic effects.

Uric acid is yet another major antioxidant which is present in our blood and saliva. There is one hypothesis that the uric acid in our blood is responsible for the fact that we have extended our lifespan when compared with other mammals.

Cabbage is an edible plant that contains phenols that are said to confer inhibition of carcinogenises. As a child I could never stomach cabbage and often I remember my mother insisting "eat this" (shoving a cabbage on a fork in my direction and showing the whites of her eyes from time to time) "it's good for you." My unprintable, unspeakable response was drowned in an orgy of sobbing and snuffling. However, decades later it can now be reported that I actually like cabbage and eat it on a fairly regular routine. Incidentally, my mother was very fond of "cabbage water." This is the liquid residue after the cabbage boiled. She used to drink it (how simply awful!) every other day or so. My mother is still going strong at 90 years of age and has not been sick in my memory, although she has had an operation for cataracts.

My Own Diet

The message is a clear one: the food that
we eat is a major, if not the primary, deter-
minant in aging and health. That being so,
what are we going to do about it? The
bookshelves in the stores are replete with all
manner of texts on this or that diet and I am
not going to go into competition with those
worthies. Instead, the following will be a more
or less trivial account of what I eat *every other
day*.

It is necessary to recognize that breakfast
is the most important meal of the day. If you
stock up then, the engine can run on the
results for the remainder of the day. A nice
advantage for the slimmers amongst you is
that whilst you are burning up the energy
made available from breakfast, you are not
storing it up as fat. I eat no lunch, not even
free ones. Dinner is an average meal except
for the fact that it is the main family and
social meal of the day. The eating routine is
therefore:
• a big breakfast
• skip lunch
• eat a normal dinner

My Don'ts

First, a list of those things I do not eat or drink. I drink coffee and tea only occasionally and also alcoholic beverages from time to time, but all three infrequently. I never eat fried food and I wouldn't be caught dead eating a hamburger or any of its other relatives. I never (Never? Well, hardly ever) use salt or pepper and rarely eat spiced food. Mushrooms are not a favorite of mine so they only become part of my diet on two or three occasions each year. At one time I tried a diet that consisted almost entirely of legumes — peas, beans and lentils. The diet was healthy enough, but eventually it came to an end because it was so very boring. If you don't believe me, try eating a legume diet for 7 months. It's enough to send one to the funny farm. Yet, on another occasion my wife and I ate Heinz Baked Beans for 12 months. This occurred because we had borrowed money from the bank to buy our first home. In a fit of unbelievable stupidity, I promised to pay the cash back in 12 months. As we were newly married, we knew very little about looking after ourselves properly. Gradually as the year wore on we both looked with increasing hatred at the "beans". But we survived, paid off the loan in 12 months, and acquired a friend at the bank. (How many people can boast that they have a friend at the bank?) The funny thing is that from time to time I still eat beans out of the can! But I eat broad beans only three or four times a year. I never did like mustard, nor horseradish and in my book spiced tea is best left for little old ladies to drink. One can take precautions against foods molding by buying from reputable shops and by being careful to avoid off-looking produce and by being a little fussy by *not* purchasing damaged fruit and vegetables (remember the little killer browned-off spud?) It also pays dividends to clean out your refrigerator on a regular basis. Otherwise you may be surprised as to what lives in there. As I eat no fried food, we do not keep cooking fat in the house. But if you do deep pan fry, etc., make sure you throw out old fat lest it goes rancid. In any case, do not keep cooking fat too long because it will go bad. Back to my habits again, I eat neither butter nor margarine. I do not like the latter and can live without the former. My main weakness is for sweet stuff. I like cakes, candy, cookies. You name it, I like it. This causes problems. The head of the U.S. Food and Drug Administration felt it necessary to defend sugar and dispel a scurrilous rumor by announcing that apart from tooth rot, sugar is not a health hazard. It is a problem if you are a diabetic. Despite this, there is a puritan streak in most of us, and in consequence, many self-opinionated people express the opposite view to the FDA chief. Perhaps they are trying to get their names in print. And, just maybe they are right. However, I prefer to believe the FDA 'cause I like sweets. The upshot of this is that I eat a lot of goodies that may contain cottonseed oil or other oils (read the labels). And, of course, I eat a fair amount of sugar. You will see, therefore, that my normal dietary habits evade the eating of many items in Table 1. I know what you are thinking! But there is something that you did not know; the items in Table 1 are only a sample of all the nasties in our food. There are many more. So, despite being cautious, you can be sure that I am surely eating harmful substances. I wonder what they are?

Breakfast

Usually for breakfast for the main dish I eat fish which is cooked in the microwave oven under a little plastic wrapper. It is important to obtain fish that is not tainted with mold in any way. (I suspect that the stomach cancers of Japan are due to the incidence of fish mold — totally unproven.) Rather than buy the "fresh" fish, we buy frozen fish. One has to be careful with this because some of these appear to be soaked in water that was far from fresh before being frozen. On the breakfast plate, along with the fish are fruit and vegetables including carrots, tomatoes, onions, peppers, apples, kiwi, cucumbers and anything else that is handy. All of these items are raw except for the cooked fish. The main dish is preceded by cereal and followed by toast. The outline is as follows:

- Bran cereal with apple and banana. Whole cream milk.
- Fish dish with fruits and vegetables.
- Toast made from pumpernickle bread and either cheese or marmalade.

From time to time the urge for variety creeps in. The main dish may then be replaced with scrambled egg into which all of the fruit and vegetables are chopped up. Every now and then I may eat a chicken or just plain vegetable and fruit as the main dish. Sometimes this is so good one does not miss the fish, egg or chicken.

On the days that I eat, just to be sociable, I will have a dish of soup at lunchtime. But this is not often.

Dinner

For the evening meal, the pattern depends upon the time of year. Generally in the winter soup is available and there is a stew season which coincides with the very bitter cold weather of January and February. For many years I used to eat steak for dinner along with some raw vegetables and fruit as at breakfast. However, more recently more adventure has crept in. Sometimes I now eat chicken instead of beef. Oh! I forgot to mention, I *never* eat pork chops, ham or anything else that has to do with those little animals. When away on a trip, I may sometimes eat bacon just to remember what it tastes like (I like it). But, on the whole, this is one idea that the Moslems have really got right. They believe that pork is unclean, and when you see hogs roaring around on the farms, who can doubt it. As time goes by, the amount of meat in the evening meal declines. Also, I tend to eat some cooked vegetables in the evening such as broccoli, spinach, cabbage, celery, beans, and peas to mention the ones that come to mind at the moment.

Enjoy

Apart from the heavy dose of sweet stuff, the above is a fairly healthy and balanced (in both senses) diet. It will not have escaped your notice that by eating it only every other day, one can literally spend twice as much per meal as one otherwise would. This tends to ensure the higher quality of what one eats, which is no bad thing.

In normal circumstances I never deviate from the above routine. I rarely eat out at restaurants because they usually serve fried rubbish at the price I would pay. The more expensive ones in the area where I live are mostly not worth visiting. It has been my unpleasant experience that usually when I am trying to be nice to a friend or a relative by offering them a celebration meal at a restaurant, the establishment fails dismally. This is unfair on three counts — it is a waste of time and money, it hurts the guest, and most important of all, I cannot scream at the head waiter because I am on my best behavior due to the presence of my guest. All the same, I told the last place to take the chef out and shoot him. The funny thing is that they thought I was joking.

To conclude the dissertations on diet — I have presented the above information and fixations to help determine what I eat. After a lot of experimenting, the above represents what I believe to be a quite healthy diet that hopefully is not increasing my rate of aging and probably holds it in check somewhat. Even with the sweets and the like, it is certainly not a fattening diet. I am about one half of an inch over six feet tall and weigh 180 lbs. At one time, some 25 years ago, I increased to 216 lbs. mainly due to the consumption of ice cream (I used to go for a walk in the lunch hour with a colleague and we bought an ice cream each. I looked like a puffing billy.) It was a very enjoyable diet. I love eating.

Perhaps it would be much more pleasant to have some very fancy dishes every now and then. However, I do not feel comfortable eating food that hides what it is that you are eating. If I am eating carrots, then they have to look and taste like carrots so I am definitely not a romantic when it comes to food. I do my experimenting while traveling and even then I'm careful, if not prudent. Things I avoid like the plague are ground beef, pizza, smoked meats, and sausage. I also avoid sauces out of bottles. It really sounds dull, but the taste of really fresh food the way the good Lord made it is an unbeatable experience that we only have one shot at. I firmly believe that it reduces your rate of aging too. Your problem is to sort out your own diet so that you are satisfied that it helps the rate of your aging process(es). Good luck.

VI. Vitamins and Minerals

It pays to be cautious . . . Hopefully.

People have written great learned tomes about vitamins and how wonderful they are. Yet others rail against taking any supplementary vitamins, pronouncing that old adage "there's no scientific proof." That may be so, and they might be right, but I still feel just a little bit unsure as to whether I should take supplemental vitamins or not. Therefore, I have worked out a compromise. I take them until the proof arrives. If I sense that they harm me, or if some information turns up that is negative, then I change the policy *tout suite*. The list is below:

• *Vitamin E*, 400 IU daily at breakfast (all vitamins are taken at this time.) The form is alpha tocopherol. There is one noticeable effect: if I do not take Vitamin E, there seems to be a slight problem with getting enough oxygen during the daily run.

However, this may be purely psychological.

- *Vitamin C,* 1 gram in the form of ascorbic acid. I used to take three grams per day as Linus Pauling suggests (he actually recommends much more than this each day). But he and his former assistant have had an argument and a lot of negative things were stated. My impression was that there was an implication that excess vitamin C was in some way connected with stomach trouble. At that time I reduced from 3 grams to 1 gram. My feeling is that it isn't enough, but it pays to be cautious until one finds out otherwise.

- *Zinc,* 60 mg in the form of zinc gluconate. There is some conflicting information on the role of zinc in the body. It is known that it is an essential component in many reactions in the body. But some reports indicate it assists cancers to develop once they have got going. It is supposed to be good for the prostate and I can report no problems there since taking zinc. This was not always the case. I think that cutting out coffee drinking was a smart move in this direction too.

- *Selenium,* 50 mcg per dose is included in the diet since a friend and neighbor of mine developed colon cancer which spread. It is important not to take too much selenium because it is toxic in too high a dose. I take it every other day.

- *Vitamin A,* 5,000 IU and *Vitamin D,* 400 IU — both from halibut liver oil. One cannot always have carrots or tomatoes at a meal. Also, the sun does not shine every day for the vitamin D.

- *Niacin,* 100 mg, sometimes 50 mg. The most notable effect of this is that it expands the blood vessels in the skin for a short while. I reckon that a nice blush once a day is no bad thing for one's skin. I read somewhere that niacin in too high a dose can damage the kidneys.

- *Choline,* 250 mg; *inositol,* 250 mg and *PABA* (para amino benzoic acid). These substances have been variously reported in the literature as useful in the treatment of aged patients. I believe that some success with Parkinson's disease has been observed. Memory is said to be improved by some. My own experience has been quite surprising and positive. At one time I had difficulty remembering *for sure* all sorts of telephone numbers. Within two weeks of starting up the choline/inositol/PABA dose it became much easier to remember the numbers. Now I take it daily.

• *Vitamin B* complex plus Vitamin B$_{12}$, 1 mg are included as a precaution. I have found that B$_{12}$ gives a noticeably improved feeling of zip during the course of a day. I take both of these vitamin sources only on the days when I eat.

To summarize, the make-up of the vitamin and mineral program is shown in Table 2.

Table 2
VITAMIN AND MINERALS SUPPLEMENTS IN DIET *

	Eating Days	Fasting Days
Vitamin E	x	x
Vitamin C	x	x
Zinc	x	-
Selenium	x	-
Vitamens A and D	x	x
Niacin	x	x
Choline/Inositol/PABA	x	x
Vitamin B Complex	x	-
Vitamin B$_{12}$	x	-

From time to time I have experimented with taking *calcium,* but after four trials I have given it up. The main reason for this was that there occurred a build-up of calcification (or something!). The effect of calcification was to cause pain in the left arm (which messed up my piano playing for a few weeks) and in both hip joints. Since stopping calcium, these effects have gone away.

Regarding the B_{12}, an 85-year-old friend of my wife has also found that this vitamin gives her a lot of extra zip during the day. I cannot recommend the taking of supplemental vitamins because I cannot be bothered to go through the voluminous literature to obtain data to support the recommendations. Therefore I have stated above what I take as part of the ARR program. As in the other parts of the program, you will have to make up your own mind what to do and experiment in order to find out what is best for you.

VII. Exercise
Running

I run every day about 3-4 miles and love every minute of it. Upon looking back to try to determine when the habit started, it came to me as a surprise when I realized that my daily run had started at the age of 9½. Our home was 2½ miles from school, and to get there on time I had to run. The running habit continued until the first major change in lifestyle occurred when I went off to work in industry. During that 5-year period, I became so out of shape that one day our 6½-year-old daughter beat me in a race around the park. Since that time I have run regularly. Over the years the distance has varied all the way up to 12 miles per day. Too long a distance results in unwelcome wear and tear on the body and can also make injuries more likely. As the idea is to keep on running, it seems prudent not to overdo it; however, you must see that I am sold on running.

Running and Aging

What of the effect of running on the rate of aging and also on the health in general? Despite all of the research, there is probably one set of evidence that says running is no good and another set that says running is wonderful for you. One really must believe the evidence of one's own experience in such matters. I believe that each day that I run is a day that I will not die on (at least not by natural causes). I look forward to my daily run with great and pleasurable anticipation. There is no doubt whatsoever in my mind that running has helped maintain good health, a good attitude, and a feeling of not being old. This is not exactly a feeling of being youthful, because that would be ridiculous at 54. However, I do not feel old or older and my reaction to the phrase "middle-age" is a simple cringe. If I was not able to perform the physical act of running, then I would feel seriously disadvantaged if not disenfranchised. On the occasions when I have been injured and unable to run, I envy those who do run and begin to feel more somber and serious. Altogether not a state of being that I enjoy.

Perhaps one day when I can no longer run, I will not want to. That will be more acceptable. My conclusion is that running helps reduce my rate of aging. It is therefore central to ARR.

Other Benefits

Are there any other ways of exercising other than running? For me, no. For you — that is for you to determine. One thing for sure, you have to have an aerobic exercise. It is vital that your heart and lungs be involved in a considerable effort. Their exercise each day keeps them in good shape and helps your body to face life's challenges.

Every five years I start a weightlifting routine — nothing heavy, just fairly light weights. This routine is carried on for a year and a half. After that it gets boring, so I quit. This weightlifting tones up the muscles and I believe helps reconstitute and unwrangle all the snarled-up tissue.

There are other and deeper benefits to running. One important one is that by the very process of forcing yourself to run, your system will quickly come to heel and achieve a high

71

level of coordination. In my own case, if I don't run in the morning it takes the rest of the day for my system to sort itself out and even by nightfall I'm still not working in one piece. The run clicks everything into line. It takes at least a mile to start to achieve this coordination.

One very substantial yet immeasurable benefit of running is the opportunity it affords for introspection. One can journey effortlessly through that world of unseen visions and unheard silences, through that insubstantial country of the mind. It is very difficult to accurately describe what one thinks about when running. In my case, I have found that thoughts whiz this way and that, such that decisions are made and also some good ideas arise from time to time. Probably the average runner would be hard put to say what he or she thinks about when running, but the decisions made and the ideas generated indicate that something is going on out there.

Each and every day our living time is begged, borrowed, and stolen from us by others. Some pay us cash, some in kind, and some don't pay at all. The result is that by the evening we have waltzed through a day, but others have used our life . . . time. The latter is a consumable. It can never be borrowed, only taken. My morning run takes about 20-25 minutes. Dressing takes 5-10 minutes depending on whether it is winter or summer. Undressing takes 5 minutes, including hanging up the kit ready for the next time out. This means I have the first half hour of my life as time each and every day for myself. Once it has been consumed, neither you, nor anyone else can take it from me. I have discovered by this stratagem I never begrudge my time to another during the remainder of the day. I got the first and best part of the day.

In the early days of the fasting routine, I would often feel a little bit weak in the morning after the fasting day and before the breakfast. This rarely bothers me now, so I suppose that the system has adjusted over the course of time. To summarize the advantages I get from a daily run:
- It keeps me fit.
- It helps me maintain a good attitude.
- It keeps me feeling not old and not older, if not actually feeling younger.
- It helps me feel as though I'm a winner. (After all, I just ran three miles, didn't I?)

- It aids coordination of my system.
- It ensures that 30 minutes of each day is reserved for my exclusive use.

    That's not a bad set of benefits for something that is free.

VIII. Stress Control
Stress is Necessary

Some people believe that stress is harmful and that every effort should be made to reduce its intensity on us. The idea then goes on to imply that once protected against stress we will flourish like little flowers, eventually becoming what the divinity intended us to be. To this and similar meanderings, I say "Bunkum!" The whole history of our species and indeed our successful evolution has been one long and arduous reaction to stress. Without stress, we would not be here, there would not be any homo-sapiens. But there are different kinds of stress. The one to avoid is the one that one cannot respond to. If you get caught in an alley by a group of muggers and they knock the tar out of you, that is a damaging stress. Alternatively, if you get away before they lay a finger on you, that is a stress that need not be avoided. By escaping you do not actually get beaten up, which is good. Also, by escaping you live to fight another day. And more especially you learn from the experience and hopefully avoid another similar confrontation in the future.

Good and Bad

Stress causes damage. If the damage can be repaired in the normal course of your life without any special and unusual response on your part, and if you can actually learn from the experience or achieve your intended goal, then the stress is an acceptable type of stress. Otherwise you have to take evasive action.

Think of an extreme example. You have been captured and are being tortured for some information which *you do not have.* The villain keeps on pulling out fingernails and asking his questions. No matter what you say or do, he will not believe that you do not have the information that he seeks. The stress level on you will rise and the damage will accumulate. This is an unacceptable stress. On the other hand, if he tortures you until you tell him what he wants to know and then he stops the torture and maybe even lets you go, this is an acceptable stress. It's not nice, but it's tolerable. These serve as two examples, one at each end of the scale. In reality there are all types of stress, covering the whole scale from one end to the other.

Stress Management

So, we cannot avoid stress. Stress is nature's way of telling us something. But can we manage it? Of course we can. There are numerous fine books and even courses of instruction on the subject. Rather than go through a lot of that sort of information, let us review the method that I use to try to reduce the stress that I experience in daily life.

In a simplistic way, one can say that there are two parts to our lives, the public and the private. The family life is the private side and our life in the work place is our public side. There is no way that we are going to discuss the problems of marriage and family life except to pass on the thought that was passed on to me from whom I know not: if you cannot keep your wife satisfied, then you are in big trouble. If you should decide to develop your own ARR program and you do not go overboard about it and exhaust yourself, you should have no trouble keeping your loved one in a positive frame of mind. Sure, one has squabbles, rows, some shouting and a little stiffness now and then, but two active, lively and energetic lovers are bound to fight from time to time. The big trick is not to so stress the other party or oneself such that any permanent damage occurs. Knowing how to cope with the stress in the work place depends on the type of job one does. In my case, I deal with a lot of people mostly with little or no major problems. I believe this is because I reduce my frustration level to a bare minimum. This is achieved by having lots of irons in the fire. Thus, I always have a lot of projects going on. If projects 1, 2, 3, and 4 are playing up today, then I shift on to projects 5, 6, 7 and 8 and so on. By adopting this technique, I reduce my level of frustration. In turn this allows me to avoid venting frustrations on others. For example, if Joe has not got his project to the stage we want it at (or to the stage it should be at), I don't start screaming at poor old Joe. I merely let Joe exit and get back to his project, then I talk to Bill about his project. During the course of the day, there will always be some success. Therefore, I win a little every day.

Winning

It is very important to feel like a winner each and every day. People like to be around a winner. If you structure your work in your mind so that at least some portion of your efforts during the day is successful, you will gradually learn how to be a winner and your behavior will modify accordingly. Mine did. It is an extremely successful method of reducing stress. A winner does not feel very much stress, he just breezes along regardless. "Whoa!" you might say, "That is self-delusion. You are not a real winner!" My response to that is that most of the things that go on in our lives during the course of the day are going on in our minds. Is that real? My technique has created reality for me because it builds success. It does not make an illusion, it makes the real thing.

I therefore manage my frustration (which is stress on me) by always, *always* having a lot of things going on all at the same time. It's a bit like being on a race track with no pit stops. The race has been going on for years now and I love it, every minute of it.

Yet another way of reducing stress is to operate in such a way that you generate a bigger bang for the buck. This is so-called leverage. In short, one assiduously pursues the path of high productivity. This again helps to make one feel like a winner. And a winner doesn't feel pain as a loser does. That is to say the stress level is apparently reduced in the case of the winner. Please note that we are *not* talking about competition. Just because Mr. A is a winner does not mean to say that Mssrs. B and C have to be losers. All three can feel like winners and be perceived as ones, too. The essential behavior that flows from such a winning M.O. is one of cooperation rather than competition. Cooperation helps make even the little people feel like winners and *we like it.* It modifies behavior and further helps to reduce the stress level on oneself — not to avoid the stress itself, but to make it more manageable.

Planning

Another major technique that helps reduce stress in quite a surprising way is that of planning. By this is meant planning one's personal life. The first time I tried this technique, it was a spectacular success. I made a five-year plan. To do this, I looked into the future and figured out where I wanted to be in five years' time. Then I developed the fourth year of the plan. After this, the third year was planned — the second year, and finally I got around to the first. As the first year of the plan appeared to be achievable, I assumed that the remainder of the plan was ok, too. Needless to say, the plan was successful and every objective was met with the exception of one. And on that one, I had changed my mind after the second year. To have a plan and to achieve its goals is a fine thing, and it certainly helps to make one feel successful.

Following a personal plan as just outlined has one important and surprising advantage. All of us have enemies. These are people who for one reason or another dislike us and behave adversely toward us. If the planner is sufficiently adroit, it is possible to co-opt a portion of the enemies' offensives and make use of them in one's own plan. For example, say that your adversary is trying to accomplish three goals. He believes that all three of them will hurt you and perhaps benefit him. Little does he know that you have a plan. If you now review your plan, you may find that one of *his* goals is one of yours also! In this case, you may be able to fight the good fight and end up with a score that appears 2-1 for him, but is actually 1-2 for you! Not only that, by knowing better what you are about than your adversary, you are much more relaxed than he thinks you should be. If you are really lucky, it is sometimes possible to end up with a score of 0-3 for you, whereas your adversary thinks it is 3-0 for him. In this case, he will be suspicious. If you continue to repeat this pattern, your adversary will get madder and madder, but he will not really know why. A variation of this technique is to yield the point to your enemy, but force him to pay dearly in different coin. This is especially relaxing for you, if such payment is delayed somewhat.

Having a large number of projects is a principle, and so is planning. Each person has to be able to decide for himself to what extent he will use these two. In my case, it has been very successful.

The Work Ratio

One source of potential stress that bothers every productive person from time to time is the work ratio. This is illustrated as follows: in every group of ten employees, about two on average are working while the other eight just seem to float around in a semi-torpor of feeble idleness. (Maybe I'm being too harsh?) True, every now and again there is a directive from on high, but there is no guarantee that the bolt of lightning will only strike the eight, because it just as easily might hit one of the two productive people. But on the whole, the operation just chugs away with two doing the work of ten. The interesting thing is that if either of the two productive ones flag or otherwise lose interest in what they are doing and their productivity drops — say to that of the other eight in the group — then the eight will fall on the recently productive person like a ton of bricks. As they used to say, it's like the pot calling the kettle black. It is hypocritical but it happens. It is not fair but that does not stop it from occurring. Now, most productive people know that the situation described is similar, if not identical, to their own. If you are one of these, just learn to accept it. For, in fact, you are something of a champion in your little group. You may not receive the pay nor the local recognition because you are in the minority, but rest assured that they depend on you. Hold onto this thought because it is the only comfort that you're going to get. I have experienced the frustration of this problem. Various authors ascribe it as being due to "group dynamics," others to poor management. Whatever the cause, one accepts it as the norm. In this way, I have avoided a stress due to frustration about something that I can do absolutely nothing about.

Conflict

Being a winner isn't all a bed of roses. It has its problems and some of the more serious ones focus around people. We deal with people at home, at work, in social contexts. A great deal of stress is generated when people interact. It helps to divide those that one meets into three groups — friends, enemies, and everybody else. The first group includes people ranging all the way from very close friends to those ones acquainted with in a friendly way. It tends to be a rather small group. Hopefully, the group labeled enemies is a very small one. All the same, it is important to *know your enemies*. If you know who they are, you can try to anticipate their moves against you. With a bit of practice you can eventually reduce the stress they impose on you and, with luck, you can effectively manage the rest of it. Once you have identified your enemies and developed methods of stress management, you should include their persons and their influences in your plans. Just because you don't like them, and they seem to hate you, you must not ignore them; don't pretend that they are not there because they are. It is also necessary to soberly consider whether or not to take action against enemies. For my part, I have always been careful to recognize that *I should not engage in battle unless I am prepared to lose the war.* This is the cardinal rule when dealing with enemies. Another way of saying it is don't start something that you are not prepared to finish. An enemy may keep pressing despite what one does to avoid conflict. At some stage in this situation, one has to decide either to quit and leave the field for good, or to fight a battle. If the decision is to fight, it is necessary to plan the war at that time. I have discovered that enemies usually (but not always) work on the assumption that most people are afraid of conflict. If one is not afraid of conflict, this fact is a double advantage to one over one's enemy. Enemies do not necessarily have to be nasty people, but mine mostly have been really horrid types. It has been my observation that such as these almost always tend to assume that the adversary is stupid. This again is a tremendous double advantage. (That is, assuming one is not stupid!)

High Productivity and Winning

My hypothesis is that the best way to reduce, contain and cope with stress is to be a winner. Winners do not feel pain to the same extent that losers do, and therefore, it is my hypothesis that winners suffer less damage. I believe that they age less rapidly as a result. How do we define a winner? My definition is that a winner is a person with a high productivity. There are three major factors that influence productivity. These are:
• Interest

- Drive
- Ability

An individual's productivity is the product of these three. For example, assuming that each component can have a maximum value of 3, this yields a productivity of 3 x 3 x 3 = 27. Assuming the average person has a component average value of 1.5 yields a productivity of 1.5 x 1.5 x 1.5 = 3.375. I know people who are very smart and intelligent, but they are not very interested in doing anything or they have a low drive, or they just don't have the requisite skills for the task at hand. In any of these cases, the person's productivity will be low for the reasons stated. Each of the above three factors has a corresponding genetic potential and an environmental influence which is to say that both nature and nurture play a great role in determining the three.

I divide life into three stages. The first twenty-five years mostly consists of acquiring skills. The second twenty-five years involves most of us in working very hard to achieve success. In the third twenty-five years we hope to get the crop in, to harvest the results of our efforts. Therefore, in the first twenty-five years, productivity is not a major concern because in that period we are getting our education and training. Most of us have only the vaguest idea as to what our future work will entail, but we make the choice of the future career at an early age nevertheless. This means that during our working lives, we adapt our behavior to suit our need to work at something. So our interest in what we do for a living can develop to quite a high level. An individual's drive is quite different from the other two factors. I believe that it is a product of the living experience of the person, especially family life and background. All the same, a person has to have some innate personal drive: otherwise there is nothing to build on. One cannot increase something that isn't there in the first place. I do not believe that added drive can be taught to a willing subject. It is effectively learned when the subject can see that it pays off with success. To summarize: education, training and background all play a major role in developing the three factors of productivity: in my own case, I have a high drive, above average ability, and above average interest with an estimated productivity of 18. My productivity has the drive component as the major factor. When I started to feel complacent as described earlier in this book, my drive fell with shattering speed. I estimate that productivity fell to a value of 6 or 7, which is still way above average, but is actually a disastrous drop for me. I was virtually incapacitated. It was a very frightening experience. Friends who have retired tell me that they eventually experience a loss of both ability and interest.* This indicates that once one ceases to practice whatever skills one has acquired in life, one loses that ability thereafter. What seems to happen is that a retired individual toys with the idea of "doing something," but as time passes he or she loses confidence that they can perform adequately. Once this stage is reached, the remaining skills quickly atrophy.

So, being productive is like playing the piano — if you don't do your practice, you will not acquire the necessary skills, and once acquired, if you do not continue to play you will soon enough lose whatever skill that you had. I always strive to increase my productivity. It is a sort of game. Translated into other terminology, I try to make a bigger bang for the buck.

To Summarize the Chapter

I do not avoid stress; rather, I welcome it because without it I would probably achieve nothing, go nowhere, meet no one, produce nothing, have a low self-esteem, and be a most irksome person to all others. Without stress I would be a failure; there would be no success in my life. I would be an unattractive person of no account to anyone. To cope with stress by managing it means to use techniques to co-opt stress to one's own use, to minimize stress and also to counteract it. If someone is pulling for you, then you push. Some of the more useful ideas that I have utilized, include:

• Learn to be a winner.
• Increase and maintain high productivity.
• Operate with a large number of simultaneous projects.
• Use planning, start with a five-year plan (written).
• Co-operate with others.
• Use a resolved component of your enemy's energy for your own purposes.
• Accept the fact that you have to support the consumers in your organization.

- Know your enemies.
- Don't start a battle unless you are prepared to lose the war.
- Keep on the track, steer as well as you can, and keep your foot on the accelerator!

Finally, although I have no analytical or objective data to support my opinion, it being entirely subjective, I believe that being truthful to all and also being loyal to one's friends helps to maintain a tolerable level of stress and self-respect. At the very least, it assists one to lead a less-complicated life than might otherwise have been the case.

---

* Other values replace, in the retired person, the values so insistent in the productive person. But the retired person can continue to live intensely, if he so chooses.

IX. Funny Habits?

No funny habits? We all have some. Mine seems to be eating a lot of sweet stuff. From time to time I go on a fairly strict regime and eat only such foods at the weekend for one day (either Saturday or Sunday, depending on which day I am eating). But some people have much more serious odd habits than that.

If you have a serious and bad habit like excessive drinking, taking drugs, smoking, or even driving too fast, perhaps you should take counseling. Alternatively, you could try a technique that I have experienced. Say, for example, you like to drink but it does not agree with you. In order to reduce your imbibing it is necessary that you modify or change your behavior. An easy method is to determine that you will drink only on special occasions. For example, when you are watching the Super-bowl at home (or the Test Match or the really special event of the year for you, whatever it is). If you make your mind up to drink then and only then, two things will happen. First, you will not have stopped drinking, only cut it down. Second, you will experience pleasurable anticipation at the prospect of a really good bash on the day the Superbowl is on the telly. Third, you will actually be able to enjoy drinking for awhile. This type of procedure may seem strange at first, but if you think about it, it allows you to have your cake and eat it too. I have used the technique with great success years ago when I was trying to stop smoking. What have you got to lose?

Every now and again, one sees a poor unfortunate who has overdone it sunbathing. All leathery skin and aged beyond its years. Some of the sights are really pathetic. There, one thinks, but for the grace of God go I. That's as may be, but don't expect sunbathing less than such an extreme is without cost. The sun up in the sky so bright is the closest unshielded thermonuclear-cum-fission reactor in our part of the universe. It is agreed that one obtains vitamin D from sunlight but there is a cost in the form of radiation damage to the tissues of the body. So, again, moderate your meetings with the sun. If you must work out there a lot, use some high quality block out.

John Keith Beddow, Ph.D.

96

X. Benedicite

W ell, there you are. You now know my efforts to reduce my rate of aging. Is there a principle involved here? Yes, there is and it is this: *look after your immune system and it will look after you.* To make it a bit more personal, look at it this way. The little defenders within the body variously called macrophages, T-cells, B-cells and the like actually work for me. They are virtually my employees! Some of them are long-term employees, actually living and working for twenty years. It boils down to this: if one makes the effort to make their job easier, then surely they will be enabled to accomplish their tasks more efficiently and effectively. Their purpose in life is to defend me. This is surely a worthy cause. It must be to my benefit to give them every assistance possible. Would I do less for a human being that worked for me?

I help my internal employees function better by attempting to reduce the amount of work they have to do. This not only makes it more probable that whatever nasty things go wrong within my system can be put right, it also makes it more likely that my internal employees will police their own ranks more effectively and remove damaged and dead individuals more promptly. This means that my immune system will be in much better shape than it might otherwise have been and therefore, it ought to be able to work much more effectively.

To summarize the program of Aging Rate Reduction:
• Fast regularly
• Eat non-injurious food
• Take daily vitamins and minerals
• Aerobic exercise daily, in my case running
• Control the stress on yourself
• No funny habits

I leave the best one to the last — find a good woman that you love, marry her, remain faithful and stay happy.

By the way, if I'm right, I shall be here at 2017 at 85 years of age. Let's meet then. Otherwise, I will have missed a lot of hot dinners and the pleasure of your company. Tut!

XI. But, Seriously, What If . . .?

W hat if it does not work — the aging rate reduction. I mean, won't the effort described in this book have been a waste?

The answer in its simplest form is *no?*

There are two major rewards if one follows the regimen outlined in this book. Both rewards substantially improve the quality of one's life. They are concerned with the improved self-image and the spiritual benefits generated within the individual.* As a result of the ARR program.

• There is a deep sense of personal well-being, increased productivity, and more happiness *now*. No one *really* knows whether living longer is beneficial, certainly it is not if one becomes a burden in any form. But feeling good physically *now*, feeling good about oneself *now*, and knowing oneself to be a success productively *now*, these are rewards and goals attainable *now*, if one makes the reasonable effort that I have suggested in this book. And, having earned these returns one may safely leave the future to itself, for one will control his life then, also, after a lifetime of self discipline.

• There are spiritual rewards to be earned and enjoyed if one follows a regimen outlined in this book. By 'spiritual' is meant the gratification from success; the feeling good about oneself, physically, intellectually, and morally; the sense of contribution to the life we live in; the thrill of achieving something we set out to do; the pleasure of the affection and respect of family, friends and acquaintances whom we care for; the felicity in loving and being loved; the very esoteric appreciation of giving, giving not someone, nor for a purpose, but just the giving of oneself to life.

'That's all very nice,'' I can hear you say, "but what about aging rate reduction?''

If there has ever been a study done concerning the relationship between a man's sense of well-being and his rate of aging, it has escaped my attention. But I would expect that miserable and unhappy people are not gifted with long life. More especially, I believe that personal neglect can only lead to self-inflicted damage and decay. Deep within ourselves we *know* that emotional, spiritual and physical depradations all interact synergestically upon us, for are we not whole? To reduce the extent and intensity of the damage is the discipline of a lifetime well spent.

* I am grateful to my friend Tom Farrell for both words and thoughts.